How to Raise and Train a
Scottish Terrier

by Robert Gannon

Photos by Louise Van Der Meid

Distributed in the U.S.A. by T.F.H. Publications, Inc., 211 West Sylvania Avenue, P.O. Box 27, Neptune City, N.J. 07753; in England by T.F.H. (Gt. Britain) Ltd., 13 Nutley Lane, Reigate, Surrey; in Canada to the book store and library trade by Clarke, Irwin & Company, Clarwin House, 791 St. Clair Avenue West, Toronto 10, Ontario; in Canada to the pet trade by Rolf C. Hagen Ltd., 3225 Sartelon Street, Montreal 382, Quebec; in Southeast Asia by Y.W. Ong, 9 Lorong 36 Geylang, Singapore 14; in Australia and the south Pacific by Pet Imports Pty. Ltd., P.O. Box 149, Brookvale 2100, N.S.W., Australia. Published by T.F.H. Publications, Inc. Ltd., The British Crown Colony of Hong Kong.

PHOTO CREDITS

The photographer is indebted to the following people for their assistance: Paul Common's TAMMY was used for the Novice Obedience photos; Mrs. Levitt's Scotties were utilized for the Advanced Obedience photos; Lena Kardos used her Champion Scotties and newborn puppies; Mrs. Serena G. Ferrer for her Wheaton Scotties and her son Bill; C.B. Van Meter also supplied Wheaton Scotties; Martha Melikov and Lorain Davis of the registered Marlorain Kennels supplied the Scotties in the grooming series; Mrs. Paula McCullough posed as a model in some photos; and Dr. Smith of Harbor Small Animal Clinic helped with the Veterinarian shots.

ISBN 0-87666-383-8

Manufactured in the United States of America
Library of Congress Catalog Card No. : 59-12997

Contents

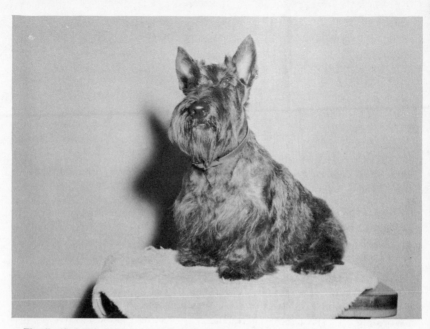

The dignified Scottie bears himself with the pride and sense of individuality native to his breed. Scotties can be very reserved, but this is most likely to occur on state occasions, such as formal portraits before the camera.

1. History of the Breed

Probably no other dog has been as publicized as that sturdy midget, the Scottish Terrier. His picture has appeared so frequently in advertisements and on everything from cocktail napkins to birthday cards that few people fail to recognize him.

One of the oldest of the Terriers (many lovers of the breed insist that the Scottie is the forerunner of all Highland Terriers), the reserved, dour and independent Scottish Terrier bears well and proudly his national origin.

His appearance may be described as quaint; yet his solid, low-set contour—something like an old-time naval gunboat—pleases the eye. When his chin whiskers are combed out his muzzle looks like a box, setting off his squarish body.

The Scottie has a gentleman's dignity and tolerance. He will remain aloof, refusing to do things he considers a frivolous waste of his time. He far prefers to rest until something really worth while comes along.

This popular breed usually is ebony (as was Fala, President Roosevelt's Scottie), but often is wheaten, gray or grizzled.

THE SCOTTIE'S BACKGROUND

Back 200 years or so Scottish Highland breeders who were not too concerned with such things as bloodlines and pedigrees tried to develop a dog that could dig like a mole, was small enough to squeeze down into the larger chuckholes and would charge into combat with all furred animals, from rats to foxes, that dwelled in the cairns—immense hills of stone scattered throughout the mountain regions of Scotland. The Scotsmen began with a large measure of the Skye Terrier (different then from today's long-haired pet) and through many cross-breedings and bloodline mixings produced a strong, fearless, typically Highland dog, the Scottish Terrier, to hunt in the cairns and accompany the district tod-hunters (tod means fox) on their rounds.

Though we have no records of the early effectiveness of this fast, brave little hunter, we can be assured that he was good, for in the old days dogs were not kept in the Highlands unless they could pay their way in hunting ability.

Some authorities say the Scottie possesses a common ancestry with the West Highland and Cairn Terriers. Some even say that Yorkshire Terrier blood is prominent in the Scottie, but this claim is more conjecture than fact.

Actually, dog experts don't agree among themselves on the history of the dogs

Scotties differ from each other in both behavior and color. Yet they all have cheerful, intelligent faces, daredevil dispositions and great sensitivity.

that come from Scotland. The early beginnings of the breeds date back to the time when man himself had only the ballad singers and wandering minstrels to record his history, and they are shrouded in mystery and mist like the mountains of the Scottie's native Highlands.

Even in the 17th century dog authorities had trouble sorting out the breeds. For example, one expert said the Scottie was "the oldest variety of the canine race indigenous to Britain." This dog, he continued, had always been known as the Skye Terrier, "although he is different from the long-coated, unsporting-like creature with which that name is now associated."

Actually, the Scottish Terrier's close resemblance to today's Cairn is due mainly to an infusion of Scottie blood into some Cairn strains.

During the latter half of the 19th century dogs known as Scotch Terriers were fairly common in Yorkshire. These dogs bore little relation to today's Scotties, but were the ancestors of our little Yorkshire Terriers, which developed from a cross between Clydesdale or Skye Terriers and Black-and-Tan Terriers.

In 1860 in Birmingham, England, the Scottish Terrier received a show classification of its own. However, for a number of years winning dogs in this category were not Scotties, but Yorkshires, Skyes and Dandie Dinmonts.

Naturally enough, Scotsmen were riled at this misuse of their breed's name, and in the late 1870's a series of letters by various patrons of the breed, pointing up the injustice and demanding recognition for the Scottie, appeared in the *Live Stock Journal.*

Finally Captain Gordon Murray, under the pseudonym of "Strathbogie," wrote a detailed description of the Scottie, which was somewhat revised to form the basis of the standard prepared by J. B. Morrison in 1880. This standard was the first for the Scottish Terrier, distinguishing it once and for all from every other breed.

In the meantime the dog was called by all sorts of other names. Highland Terrier was one; the Die-hard another. The latter name originated with George, Fourth Earl of Dumbarton, whose famous pack of little Scotties was used to rout all manner of animals on the Earl's hunting expeditions. Their determination, fearlessness and pluck were so notable that they were termed "Die-Hards." In fact, so great was this pack's reputation that the Earl's regiment, the Royal Scots, was bequeathed the name and became known as "Dumbarton's Die-hards."

Later an Aberdeen breeder called the Scottie the Aberdeen Terrier, a term which still crops up now and then. This man developed a fine line of dogs and called them Scottish Terriers until Highlanders started objecting to the name because they erroneously felt that other breeds of Terriers, such as the Dandie Dinmont, Cairn or Skye, had prior claim as the representative breed of Scotland.

Slowly however, the name Scottish Terrier settled firmly and steadily upon the head of the dog we know today, and in 1882 the Scottish Terrier Club was formed with joint officers for Scotland and England.

The Scottie's first colors were gray, wheaten, brindle and red-brindle. Today black is probably the most popular color, but in early times it was extremely difficult to fix and so didn't exist for decades.

What could be more natural for a Scottie's wardrobe than a Scottish tartan? This Highlander, wearing his Sunday best, is ready for a stroll in the brisk air.

The first recorded Scotties to come to the United States, Tam Glen and Bonnie Belle, were imported by John Naylor in 1883. In 1925 the present American standard was adopted.

Abroad the Scottie is still used occasionally to rout foxes, rodents and other creatures from their dens, but in America he is primarily a pet and a general house dog. The Scottie does very well as an apartment dweller. Ordinarily not very noisy, he can still raise an awe-inspiring commotion when an unannounced stranger sets foot on his property.

THE SCOTTIE'S PERSONALITY

The Scottish Terrier, often comical and affectionate, is always a one-man dog whose reserve and independence mark a truly Scottish disposition. His very individual personality may even go so far as to have a strong stubborn streak. His daredevil spirit charms, his perseverance and quick wit protect and interest people. There is a quality known as "Terrier character" which is inbred in any Terrier worthy of the name. This quality, a sort of dignified courage, is most marked in the Scottie. He walks with a definite swagger. He will strut up to a German Shepherd, bark in his face defiantly, and pad on his way, confident of having put the larger dog in his place.

A Scottie's pride is balanced by his tolerance, which is why he makes such a wonderful companion.

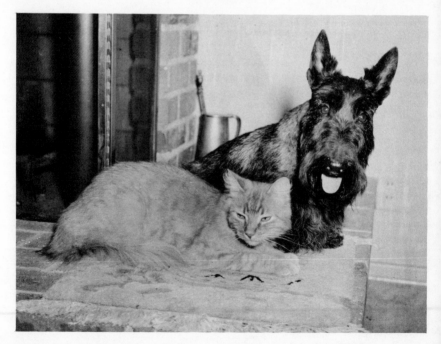

There is mutual protectiveness between these dogs and their little master. Scotties are a courageous lot, and make fine watchdogs for children.

A Scottie is an eccentric. When you buy a Scottie puppy you can never be sure what changes in temperament will come with maturity. Chances are your dog will assume a paternal air around the house, expecting you to do many foolish things, and willing to put up with all of them. A Scottish Terrier's individuality is in itself a valuable characteristic in a pet, so remember it's a wise master who lets his dog's nature develop along its own lines.

A highly sensitive animal, he hates being stared at. He seems to consider this a personal attack. If you look straight at him with a frown on your face, he will turn his head and do his best to appear indifferent.

The Scottish Terrier's ears are more expressive than most people's faces. His pert small ears are continually alert, hearing sounds which completely escape humans and telling what his mood is. One look at his ears and you'll know if he's displeased or if his feelings are hurt. They even occasionally give the impression of a wink.

STANDARDS OF THE BREED

The standards which have been adopted by the Scottish Terrier Club of America and approved by the American Kennel Club set the present-day ideal for which Scottish Terrier breeders are aiming. These are the standards by which the dog is judged in the show ring. However, even the most perfect specimen falls short of the standards in some respect. It's also impossible, even for a breeder or veterinarian, to tell how a puppy will shape up as an adult dog. The chances are that he will inherit the qualities for which his father and mother—or sire and dam in dog terminology—were bred, and if both his parents and grandparents had good show records he may have excellent possibilities.

Here, then, are the standards.

SKULL: Long, of medium width, slightly domed and covered with short, hard hair. It should not be quite flat, as there should be a slight stop or drop between the eyes.

MUZZLE: In proportion to the length of skull, with not too much taper toward the nose. Nose should be black and of good size. The jaws should be level and square. The nose projects somewhat over the mouth, giving the impression that the upper jaw is longer than the lower. The teeth should be evenly placed, having a scissors or level bite, with the former being preferable.

EYES: Set wide apart, small and of almond shape, not round. Color to be dark brown or nearly black. To be bright, piercing and set well under the brow.

EARS: Small, prick, set well up on the skull, rather pointed but not cut. The hair on them should be short and velvety.

NECK: Moderately short, thick and muscular, strongly set on sloping shoulders, but not so short as to appear clumsy.

CHEST: Broad and very deep, well let down between the forelegs.

BODY: Moderately short and well-ribbed up with strong loin, deep flanks and very muscular hindquarters.

LEGS AND FEET: Both forelegs and hind legs should be short and very heavy in bone in proportion to the size of the dog. Forelegs straight or slightly bent with elbows close to the body. Scottish Terriers should not be out at the elbows. Stifles should be well bent and legs straight from hock to heel. Thighs very muscular. Feet round and thick with strong nails, forefeet larger than the hind feet.

Note: The gait of the Scottish Terrier is peculiarly its own and is very characteristic of the breed. It is not the square trot or walk that is desirable in the long-legged breeds. The forelegs do not move in exact parallel planes—rather in reaching out incline slightly inward. This is due to the shortness of leg and width of chest. The action of the rear legs should be square and true and at the trot both the hocks and stifles should be flexed with a vigorous motion.

TAIL: Never cut and about 7 inches long, carried with a slight curve but not over the back.

COAT: Rather short, about 2 inches, dense undercoat with outer coat intensely hard and wiry.

SIZE AND WEIGHT: Equal consideration must be given to height, length of back and weight. Height at shoulder for either sex should be about 10 inches. Generally, a well-balanced Scottish Terrier dog of correct size should weigh from 19 to 22 pounds and a female, from 18 to 21 pounds. The principal objective must be symmetry and balance.

COLOR: Steel or iron gray, brindled or grizzled, black, sandy or wheaten. White markings are objectionable and can be allowed only on the chest and that to a slight extent only.

GENERAL APPEARANCE: The face should wear a keen, sharp and active expression. Both head and tail should be carried well up. The dog should look very compact, well muscled and powerful, giving the impression of immense power in a small size.

PENALTIES: Soft coat, round or very light eye, overshot or undershot jaw, obviously oversize or undersize, shyness, timidity or failure to show with head and tail up are faults to be penalized. No judge should put to Winners or Best of Breed any Scottish Terrier not showing real terrier character in the ring.

JUDGING POINTS

When comparing Scottish Terriers in the show ring, the judges rate them on the following scale of points.

Skull	5
Muzzle	5
Eyes	5
Ears	10
Neck	5
Chest	5
Body	15
Legs and Feet	10
Tail	2½
Coat	15
Size	10
Color	2½
General appearance	10
Total	100

2. Selecting Your Scottish Terrier

How much you spend for your Scottish Terrier should depend on the purpose for which you are buying him. If you are planning to show your dog, then you want a puppy with good bloodlines and the possibility of developing into a champion. This may cost several hundred dollars, and if you are not an expert on dogs, you should have an expert to help you make your selection.

If you want your Scottie to be solely a pet or companion or guard for children, you can acquire a good dog for considerably less money. The fact that his conformation may be a bit off and his ancestors weren't champions won't make him any less valuable for your purposes.

WHERE TO BUY YOUR DOG

If it is a show dog you're seeking, you'll probably do best by getting your puppy from a kennel that specializes in Scottish Terriers, or a private breeder who exhibits. If you have the chance to visit a dog show, the Scottie exhibitors there may have puppies for sale or can direct you to a good source.

If you're not so concerned about bloodlines, you can probably find the Scottish Terrier you want at a pet shop or the pet section of a department store. If you live far from any source, you can buy a Scottish Terrier by mail. Several of the larger mail order houses are in the dog business, too, and most kennels will ship a dog to you with the guarantee that the puppy is purebred and healthy.

THE PUPPY'S PAPERS

If you are investing in a purebred dog, obtain the necessary papers from the seller, especially if you are planning to show or breed your dog. Usually the litter will have been registered with the American Kennel Club. This is necessary before the individual puppy can be registered. The breeder should provide you with an Application for Registration signed by the owner of the puppy's mother. Then you select a name for your dog (it must be 25 letters or less, and cannot duplicate the name of another dog of the breed, or be the name of a living person without his written permission). Enter the selected name on the form, fill in the blanks that make you the owner of record, and send it to the American Kennel Club, 221 Fourth Avenue, New York, N.Y., with the required fee. In a few weeks if all is in order you will receive the blue and white Certificate of Registration with your dog's stud book number.

When you are ready to select your Scottie, you'll find it very difficult to make a choice from among all the lovable pups. One lively Scottie will probably come up and adopt you, instead of the other way around.

THE PEDIGREE

The pedigree of your dog is a tracing of his family tree. Often the breeder will have the pedigree of the dog's dam and sire and may make out a copy for you. Or, you can write to the American Kennel Club once your dog has been registered and ask for a pedigree. The fee depends on how many generations back you want the pedigree traced. In addition to giving the immediate ancestors of your dog, the pedigree will show whether there are any champions or dogs that have won obedience degrees in his lineage. If you are planning selective breeding, the pedigree is also helpful to enable you to find other Scottish Terriers that have the same general family background.

A HEALTHY PUPPY

The healthy puppy will be active, gay and alert, with bright, shiny eyes. He should not have running eyes or nose. If the puppy in which you are interested seems listless, it may be that he has just eaten and wants to sleep for a while. Come back for a second look in a few hours, to see if he is more active.

Remember that puppies change greatly when their second teeth come, so even though it may be all right to take a pup at the age of six weeks—when he's weaned and strong on his feet—it's a good idea to wait until about six months or so if you're primarily interested in a dog for showing.

The most important consideration in selecting a puppy is his health. Look him over carefully, examining his build, coat and general condition. It is wise to get a vet's approval, too.

A young puppy will be fat and roly-poly with a round stomach, but a ridgepole back and an excessively heavy stomach may indicate worms.

Select a short-legged but balanced puppy, one that is heavy-set and sturdy. Better bypass the runt of the litter, even though your sympathies may lie with him.

Study the coat of the puppy carefully. It should not feel silky, but quite harsh to the touch. Look for a dog with plenty of long whiskers. The puppy's head should be long, lean and powerful; not apple-shaped nor extra short. The neck should be neither too short nor thickset, but should be held gracefully. Look for ears that are snappy and upright, and a tail that's carried somewhat upright, too.

Unlike a mature Scottie, a puppy's forelegs shouldn't curve in slightly under the body, but should go straight down. On a dog of 3 months, the chest should be as low as the elbow. A young Terrier's body doesn't sit atop his legs, but is swung between them.

In buying a puppy—especially a higher-priced one—it is always wise to make your purchase subject to the approval of a veterinarian. The seller will usually allow you eight hours in which to take the puppy to a vet to have his health checked. However, come to a clear agreement on what happens if the vet rejects the puppy. It should be understood whether rejection means that you get your money back or merely choice of another puppy from the same litter.

MALE OR FEMALE?

Unless you want to breed your pet and raise a litter of puppies it doesn't matter whether you choose a male or female. Both sexes are pretty much the same in disposition and character, and both make equally good pets. The male may be a bit more inclined to roam; the female is more of a homebody. A female's daily walks needn't be as long as the male's.

If you choose a female but decide you don't want to raise puppies, your dog can be spayed and will remain a healthy, lively pet.

To weigh your dog, first weigh yourself. Then get on the scale again, this time holding your pet. Subtract your weight alone from yours and the dog's together to get your pet's weight.

Scottie puppies are particularly fine pets for a young child. They are child size and so can be easily held, and their high spirits make them amusing friends for the child to grow up with.

ADULT OR PUP?

Whether to buy a grown dog or a small puppy is another question. It is undeniably fun to watch your dog grow all the way from a baby, sprawling and playful, to a mature, dignified dog. If you don't have the time to spend on the more frequent meals, housebreaking, and other training a puppy needs in order to become a dog you can be proud of, then choose an older, partly trained pup or a grown dog. If you want a show dog, remember that no one, not even an expert, can predict with 100 per cent accuracy what a small puppy will be when he grows up.

WORMING AND INOCULATION

Before you take your puppy home, find out from the breeder if he has already been wormed or inoculated for distemper and rabies. Practically all puppies will have worms which they acquire from eating worm eggs, from fleas, or from their mother. The breeder usually gives the puppies a worming before he sells them. If yours has already been wormed, find out when and what treatment was given. The breeder may be able to advise you on any further treatment that is necessary. While there are many commercial worming preparations on the market, it's generally safer to let the vet handle it. There will be more about worms in Chapter 3.

If your puppy has been inoculated against distemper, you will also have to know when this was done so you can give the information to your vet. He will complete the series of shots. If your puppy has not yet been given this protection, your vet should take care of it immediately. Distemper is prevalent and highly contagious. Don't let your puppy out of doors until he has had his distemper shots and they have had time to take effect.

As a rule, kennels and breeders do not inoculate puppies against rabies. In some areas, rabies inoculation is required by law. However, the possibility of your dog becoming infected by rabies, a contact disease, is very slight in most parts of the country. To be perfectly safe, check with your vet who will be familiar with the local ordinances and will advise you.

While the distemper inoculation is permanent and can be supplemented by "booster" shots, rabies inoculation must be repeated yearly. When your puppy receives it, the vet will give you a tag for the dog's collar certifying that he has received the protection. He will also give you a certificate for your own records. For foreign travel and some interstate travel, rabies inoculation is required.

Once you've found the perfect pet, you're ready to take him to his new home, and a new way of life for both of you.

3. Caring for Your Scottish Terrier

BRINGING YOUR PUPPY HOME

When you bring your puppy home, remember that he is used to the peace and relative calm of a life of sleeping, eating and playing with his brothers and sisters. The trip away from all this is an adventure in itself, and so is adapting to a new home. So let him take it easy for a while. Don't let the whole neighborhood pat and poke him at one time. Be particularly careful when children want to handle him, for they cannot understand the difference between the delicate living puppy and the toy dog they play with and maul. Show them the correct way to hold the puppy, supporting his belly with one hand while holding him securely with the other.

THE PUPPY'S BED

It is up to you to decide where the puppy will sleep. He should have his own place, and not be allowed to climb all over the furniture. He should sleep out of drafts, but not right next to the heat, which would make him too sensitive to the cold when he goes outside.

You might partition off a section of a room—the kitchen is good because it's usually warm and he'll have some companionship there. Set up some sort of low partition that he can't climb, give him a pillow or old blanket for his bed and cover the floor with a thick layer of newspapers. If he seems a bit timid or retiring, get a sturdy cardboard box, cut a large door in one side and put his bed in there.

You have already decided where the puppy will sleep before you bring him home. Let him stay there, or in the corner he will soon learn is his, most of the time, so that he will gain a sense of security from the familiar. Give the puppy a little food when he arrives, but don't worry if he isn't hungry at first. He will soon develop an appetite when he grows accustomed to his surroundings. The first night the puppy may cry a bit from lonesomeness, but if he has an old blanket or rug to curl up in he will be cozy. The ticking of a clock may provide company. In winter a hot water bottle will help replace the warmth of his littermates.

Scotties—and particularly puppies—should not be housed in an outside doghouse or in the basement, unless it is exceptionally dry and warm. However, the dog will benefit from an outdoor run of his own where he can be put to

A child wants to be kind to his puppy, but he is apt to be a little rough at first. As soon as the pup comes to live with you teach your child how to handle the new pet without hurting him.

exercise and amuse himself. It does not have to be large because it will supplement his activities with you, but he will be much safer shut in his run than left loose.

FEEDING THE PUPPY

By the time a puppy is 8 weeks old, he should be fully weaned and eating from a dish. Always find out what the seller has been feeding the puppy as it is well to keep him on the same diet for a while. Any sudden change in a puppy's feeding habits may cause loose bowels or constipation.

The following feeding schedule has been used on many Scotties with good results.

WEANING TO 3 MONTHS: *A.M.*—$\frac{1}{2}$ cup of baby cereal and dog meal, mixed with warm water or milk. *Noon*—$\frac{1}{2}$ cup of warm milk, with cereal or

If you have more than one puppy, see that they all get their share to eat. Try to keep to a feeding schedule, with meals at the same time and place every day.

biscuits. *P.M.*—2 tbs. chopped beef, 2 tbs. cereal or dog meal, vitamin and mineral supplements. *Bedtime*—½ cup warm milk, mixed with ¼ cup baby cereal. Change gradually from baby cereal to dog meal.

3-6 MONTHS: *A.M.*—½ cup meat with shredded wheat or cereal. *Noon*— 1 cup milk, soft-boiled egg twice a week, or 1 cup cottage cheese. *P.M.*—½ cup meat with ½ cup dog meal; or kibble and water.

6 MONTHS-1 YEAR: *A.M.*—½ cup dog meal or cereal with cottage cheese or egg, and milk. Add vitamin and mineral supplements. *P.M.*—½ cup meat with ¾ cup kibble or meal, fat, table scraps.

OVER 1 YEAR: *A.M.*—Half of evening meal, or several dog biscuits. *P.M.*—¾ cup meat, ¾ cup dog food, mixed with meal, fat or table scraps.

ADDITIONAL FEEDING TIPS

Common sense is your best guide to feeding your Scottie. The puppy's belly should be gently rounded after eating. If he is too pot-bellied, or if he "burps" after his meal, you may be overfeeding him.

Occasional diarrhea in puppies may come from a change in food; if it persists, see your veterinarian.

Raw meat is considered better than cooked, but if your dog is ill, you should cook his meat. In any case, the food should be served at room temperature, never hot or cold.

As to the kind of meat, the lower-priced ground beef is preferable to the more expensive leaner cuts, since it contains a lot of fat that your dog needs in his diet. All kinds of liver, kidney, brains, and so forth are good. Of course you won't let your dog near chicken bones or fish with bones that can catch in his throat or tear his intestines. It is usually best not to feed him pork, fried meats or over-spiced foods.

Cream and cottage cheese are relished by most dogs and are nutritious. In addition, cottage cheese may stop mild diarrhea.

Green and yellow vegetables, cooked, are desirable dog foods, but some dogs react unfavorably to peas, onions and garlic. Cooked or raw fruit may be given, and while authorities agree that dogs do not need the Vitamin C in citrus foods, an occasional piece of orange or grapefruit may please your dog.

If you buy canned dog food, study the label carefully and make certain that it contains a large portion of meat. The lower-priced foods are frequently overloaded with cereal and are low in protein content. If you feed dried food, add beef fat or bacon drippings.

A day or two without food won't harm a healthy dog. Many kennels "starve" their dogs one day a week, claiming that this keeps them more active and alert.

A dog needs water, but don't leave a filled dish with a young puppy until he's mature enough to know it's to drink and not to swim in. Until then you can give him all he needs with his meals.

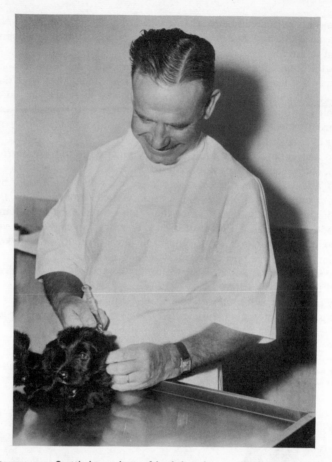

Next to you, your Scottie has no better friend than the vet, though at painful times like this a puppy is not inclined to gratitude. But it will only hurt for a second, and the shot will protect his health.

WATCHING THE PUPPY'S HEALTH

The first step in protecting the health of your puppy is a visit to the veterinarian. If the breeder has not given your puppy his first distemper shots, have your vet do it. You should also have your dog protected against hepatitis, and, if required by local law or if your vet suggests it, against rabies. Your puppy should receive his full quota of protective inoculations, especially if you plan to show him later. Select a veterinarian you feel you can trust and keep his phone number handy. Any vet will be glad to give a regular "patient" advice over the phone—often without charge.

Occasional loose bowels in a puppy generally isn't anything too serious. It can be the result of an upset stomach or a slight cold. Sometimes it will clear up in a day or so without any treatment. If you want to help the puppy's digestion, add some cottage cheese to his diet, or give him a few drops of kaopectate. Instead of tap water, give him barley or oatmeal water (just as you would a human baby). However, if the looseness persists for more than a day or two, a visit to the vet may be required. If the puppy has normal bowel movements alternating with loose bowel movements, it may be a symptom of worms.

If the puppy upchucks a meal or vomits up slime or white froth, it may indicate that his stomach is upset. One good stomach-settler is a pinch of baking soda, or about 8 or 10 drops of pure witch hazel in a teaspoon of cold water 2 or 3 times a day. In case of vomiting you should skip a few meals to give the stomach a chance to clear itself out. When you start to feed him again, give him cooked scraped beef for his first meals and then return to his normal diet. Persistent vomiting may indicate a serious stomach upset or even poisoning and calls for professional help.

WORMING

Practically all puppies start out in life with worms in their insides, either acquired from the mother or picked up in their sleeping quarters. However, there are six different types of worms. Some will be visible in the stool as small

An outdoor run of his own will allow your Scottie to exercise and amuse himself in the fresh air without any of the dangers of traffic.

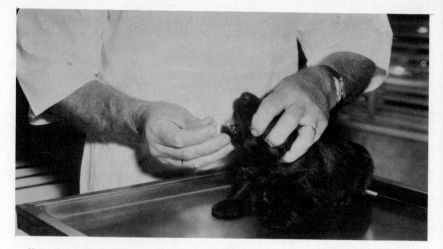

If you have any doubts about your pet's health, don't hesitate to call the veterinarian immediately. Remember the old maxim about an ounce of prevention.

white objects; others require microscopic examination of the stool for identification. While there are many commercial worm remedies on the market, it is safest to leave that to your veterinarian, and to follow his instructions on feeding the puppy before and after the worming. If you find that you must administer a worm remedy yourself, read the directions carefully and administer the smallest possible dose. Keep the puppy confined after treatment for worms, since many of the remedies have a strong laxative action and the puppy will soil the house if allowed to roam freely.

THE USEFUL THERMOMETER

Almost every serious puppy ailment shows itself by an increase in the puppy's body temperature. If your Scottie acts lifeless, looks dull-eyed and gives an impression of illness, check by using a rectal thermometer. Hold the dog, insert the thermometer which has been lubricated with vaseline and take a reading. The normal temperature is 100.6 to 101.5 (higher than the normal human temperature). Excitement may send it up slightly, but any rise of more than a few points is cause for alarm.

SOME CANINE DISEASES

Amateur diagnosis is dangerous because the symptoms of so many dog diseases are alike, but you should be familiar with most of the diseases which can strike your dog.

COUGHS, COLDS, BRONCHITIS, PNEUMONIA

Respiratory diseases may affect the dog because he is forced to live in a human rather than a natural doggy environment. Being subjected to a draft or cold after a bath, sleeping near an air conditioner or in the path of air from a fan or near a hot air register or radiator can cause one of these respiratory ailments. The symptoms are similar to those in humans. However, the germs of these diseases are different and do not affect both dogs and humans so that they cannot catch them from each other. Treatment is pretty much the same as for a child with the same illness. Keep the puppy warm, quiet, well fed. Your veterinarian has antibiotics and other remedies to help the pup fight back.

If your puppy gets wet, dry him immediately to guard against chilling. Wipe his stomach after he has walked through damp grass. Don't make the common mistake of running your dog to the vet every time he sneezes. If he seems to have a light cold, give him about a quarter of an aspirin tablet and see that he doesn't overexercise.

MAJOR DISEASES OF THE DOG

With the proper series of inoculations, your Scottish Terrier will be almost completely protected against the following canine diseases. However, it occasionally happens that the shot doen't take and sometimes a different form of the virus appears against which your dog may not be protected.

Rabies: This is an acute disease of the dog's central nervous system and is spread by the bite of an infected animal, the saliva carrying the infection. Rabies occurs in two forms. The first is "Furious Rabies" in which the dog shows a period of melancholy or depression, then irritation, and finally paralysis. The first period lasts from a few hours to several days. During this time, the dog is cross and will try to hide from members of the family. He appears restless and will change his position often. He loses his appetite for food and begins to lick, bite and swallow foreign objects. During the "irritation" phase the dog is spasmodically wild and has impulses to run away. He acts in a fearless manner and runs and bites at everything in sight. If he is caged or confined he will fight at the bars, often breaking teeth or fracturing his jaw. His bark becomes a peculiar howl. In the final or paralysis stage, the animal's lower jaw becomes paralyzed and hangs down; he walks with a stagger and saliva drips from his mouth. Within 4 to 8 days after the onset of paralysis, the dog dies.

The second form of rabies, "Dumb Rabies," is characterized by the dog's walking in a bear-like manner with his head down. The lower jaw is paralyzed and the dog is unable to bite. Outwardly it may seem as though he has a bone caught in his throat.

Even if your pet should be bitten by a rabid dog or other animal, he can probably be saved if you get him to the vet in time for a series of injections. However, by the time the symptoms appear the disease is so far advanced that no cure is possible. But remember that an annual rabies inoculation is almost certain protection against rabies.

Distemper: Young dogs are most susceptible to distemper, although it may affect dogs of all ages. The dog will lose his appetite, seem depressed, chilled, and run a fever. Often he will have a watery discharge from his eyes and nose.

Unless treated promptly, the disease goes into advanced stages with infections of the lungs, intestines and nervous system, and dogs that recover may be left with some impairment such as a twitch or other nervous mannerism. The best protection against this is very early inoculation—preferably even before the puppy is old enough to go out into the street and meet other dogs.

Hepatitis: Veterinarians report an increase in the spread of this virus disease in recent years, usually with younger dogs as the victims. The initial symptoms —drowsiness, vomiting, great thirst, loss of appetite and a high temperature— closely resemble distemper. These symptoms are often accompanied by swellings on the head, neck and lower parts of the belly. The disease strikes quickly and death may occur in a few hours. Protection is afforded by injection with a new vaccine.

Leptospirosis: This disease is caused by bacteria which live in stagnant or slow-moving water. It is carried by rats and dogs, and many dogs are believed to get it from licking the urine or feces of infected rats. The symptoms are increased thirst, depression and weakness. In the acute stage, there is vomiting, diarrhea and a brown discoloration of the jaws, tongue and teeth, caused by an inflammation of the kidneys. This disease can be cured if caught in time, but it is best to ward it off with a vaccine which your vet can administer along with the distemper shots.

External Parasites: The dog that is groomed regularly and provided with clean sleeping quarters should not be troubled with fleas, ticks or lice. However, it would be a wise precaution to spray his sleeping quarters occasionally with an anti-parasite powder that you can get at your pet shop or from your vet. If the dog is out of doors during the tick season he should be treated with a dip-bath.

Skin Ailments: Any persistent scratching may indicate an irritation, and whenever you groom your dog, look for the reddish spots that may indicate eczema or some rash or fungus infection. Do not treat him yourself. Take him to the veterinarian as some of the conditions may be difficult to eradicate and can cause permanent harm to his coat.

FIRST AID FOR YOUR DOG

In general, a dog will lick his cuts and wounds and they'll heal. If he swallows anything harmful, chances are he'll throw it up. But it will probably make you feel better to help him if he's hurt, so treat his wounds as you would your own. Wash out the dirt and apply an antiseptic or ointment. If you put on a bandage, you'll have to do something to keep the dog from trying to remove it. A large cardboard ruff around his neck will prevent him from licking his chest or body. You can tape up his nails to keep him from scratching, or make a "bootie" for his paws.

If you think your dog has a broken bone, before moving him apply a splint just as you would to a person's limb. If there is bleeding that won't stop, apply a tourniquet between the wound and heart, but loosen it every few minutes to prevent damage to the circulatory system.

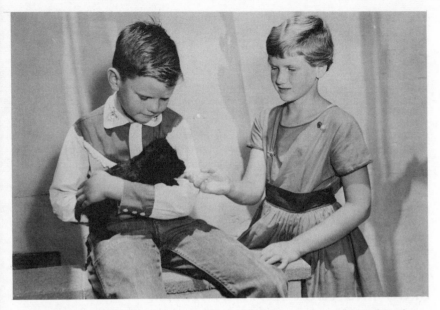

Attentive and affectionate care, a well-balanced diet and enough exercise produce the surest guarantee that your puppy will grow up to be a healthy and happy dog.

If you are afraid that your dog has swallowed poison and you can't get the vet fast enough, try to induce vomiting by giving him a strong solution of salt water or mustard in water.

SOME "BUTS"

First, don't be frightened by the number of diseases a dog can get. The majority of dogs never get any of them. If you need assurance, look at any book on human diseases. How many have you had?

Don't become a dog-hypochondriac. Veterinarians have enough work taking care of sick dogs and doing preventive work with their patients. Don't rush your pet to the vet every time he sneezes or seems tired. All dogs have days on which they feel lazy and want to lie around doing nothing.

THE FEMALE PUPPY

If you want to spay your female you can have it done while she is still a puppy. Her first seasonal period will probably occur between 8 and 10 months, although it may be as early as 6 or delayed until she is a year old. She may be spayed before or after this, or you may breed her (at a later season) and still spay her afterward.

The first sign of the female's being in season is a thin red discharge, which will increase for about a week, when it changes color to a thin yellowish stain, lasting about another week. Simultaneously there is a swelling of the vulva, the dog's external sexual organ. The second week is the crucial period, when she could be bred if you want her to have puppies, but it is possible for the period to be shorter or longer, so it is best not to take unnecessary risks at any time. After a third week the swelling decreases and the period is over for about six months.

If you have an absolutely climb-proof and dig-proof run within your yard, it will be safe to leave her there, but otherwise the female in season should be shut indoors. Don't leave her out alone for even a minute; she should be exercised only on leash. If you want to prevent the neighborhood dogs from hanging around your doorstep, as they inevitably will as soon as they discover that your female is in season, take her some distance away from the house before you let her relieve herself. Take her in the car to a nearby park or field for a chance to stretch her legs. After the three weeks are up you can let her out as before, with no worry that she can have puppies until the next season. But if you want to have her spayed, consult your veterinarian about the time and age at which he prefers to do it. With a young dog the operation is simple and after a night or two at the animal hospital she can be at home, wearing only a small bandage as a souvenir.

GROOMING YOUR SCOTTISH TERRIER

To keep your Scottie's wiry coat looking its best, you should take a few minutes every day to groom him. This will help keep his skin and coat in good condition, and a dog that is groomed regularly will seldom need a bath.

If your dog is accustomed from puppyhood to being handled, grooming should be no problem. Have him stand on a bench or platform so you won't have to do much bending down when you work on him.

CARING FOR THE COAT

Start each grooming session with a brisk rubdown with your fingertips over the dog's whole body. This will loosen any dead skin. Then give him a thorough but gentle brushing. (A bristle brush is preferable to the nylon type.) First brush his coat against the grain, then with the grain. When you brush him, especially during the summer and fall months, check his coat for any signs of fleas, lice or ticks. If you do find parasites, use a spray or dip to get rid of them. When there are fleas, you will also have to change the dog's bedding and spray the areas of the house where he stays, paying special attention to cracks in the floor and along the baseboards. Repeat the de-fleaing treatment in about a week. Make sure the dog doesn't lick too much insecticide off his coat. If necessary, you can put a clown collar around his neck so he won't be able to reach his body with his tongue. Don't leave flea powder on too long, since it may be strong enough to burn his skin or coat.

If you find ticks, be sure to remove the entire insects. You can touch them with a drop of iodine to break their grip. Then lift them off, one at a time, with a pair of tweezers or a tissue and burn them or drop them into kerosene or gasoline to kill them.

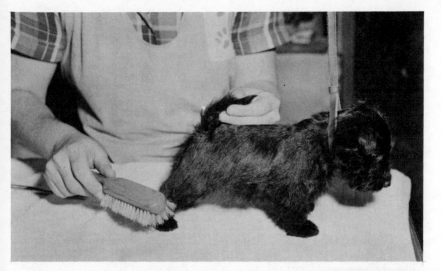

If you begin to groom your pet while he's still very young, he will come to enjoy it and look forward to the regular beauty sessions.

If you find lice, small sucking and biting insects which attach themselves to the dog's body, you must apply a good pesticide regularly, burn all the dog's bedding and thoroughly disinfect his living quarters.

When your Scottie begins to look too shaggy, it's time for a haircut. The first step in trimming is to go to a pet shop and obtain some tools made especially for his type of coat. You can also buy a trimming chart that will show you the result you will be aiming for.

Trim your Scottish Terrier with blunt scissors. Start with the skull and trim it closely. Then reduce the width of the face hair, but try to maintain a full, round look without losing any of the length of the dog's head. Leave the eyebrows fairly long—about one inch—but trim the hair between them smooth. Trim the cheeks from the outside corner of the eye to the mouth. Next, to give expression, with great care lightly trim from the inside corner of the eyes to the corner of the mouth.

The edges and backs of the ears should be trimmed fine, but don't cut the hair inside the ears. Chin whiskers should be left alone (or snipped just a bit if necessary), but the hair under the jaw from the corner of the Scottie's mouth back to the neck should be cleaned off short. Part the hair over his muzzle and comb it down and forward.

Go over the neck and back to make sure the hair is even (don't trim too finely here). Taper the tail to a point, leaving the hair heavy at its base. Cut the stern fairly close near the tail, but as you get about halfway down the ribs, leave almost all the hair, or about two inches of it, so the dog will appear close to the ground and heavy. You can leave the hair on the bottom as long as you want, trimming it only as a sanitary measure to keep it off the ground.

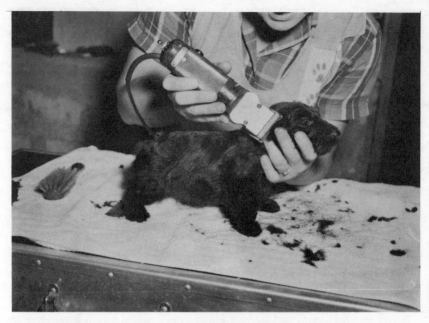

(Above) When you trim your puppy, you'll probably find that a pair of blunt scissors are easier to wield than the clippers. Shaggy dog stories are one thing, an unkempt dog another.

(Below) Your Scottie's coat should be brushed frequently, and while you're at it, check for parasites.

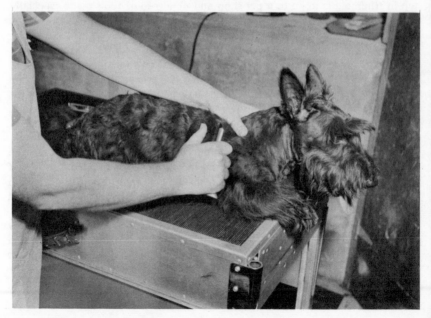

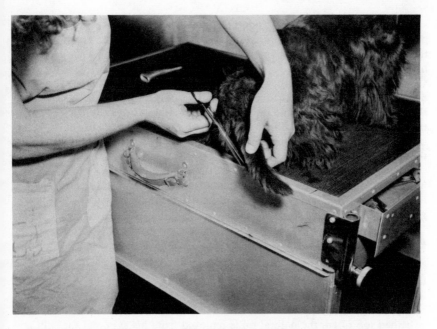

(Above) Trim the top of your dog first, beginning at the head and going down the back to the tail, which should be thick at the bottom and tapered to a point.

(Below) A brisk rubdown will loosen the dead skin and keep your Scottie's coat glowing with health.

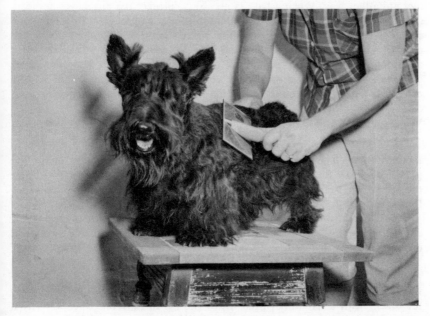

Many dogs, and particularly Scotties, must scratch when you strike certain places on their side. This reflex action makes it hard for you to comb or brush the area. If you've run into this problem, hold your dog's hind leg while grooming his side.

The hair on the front of the neck should be cut rather short, but as you work down to the brisket, leave the hair long and cut only enough so he doesn't look shaggy. Don't trim the hair on the front legs, but remove extra hair from between the toes and from the feet. Make sure the nails are cut evenly and neatly. If the legs are somewhat bent, comb the hair to make them appear straight from both the front and sides.

Go over the whole dog again to make sure no tufts or straggly hair is left to make him appear shabby. Never shorten any hair if doing so would destroy the impression that the dog is solid, of substantial breadth and is built low to the ground.

BATHING YOUR SCOTTIE

A normal, healthy dog should be bathed as *infrequently* as possible because the dog's skin is different from that of humans. It is very rich in oil glands and deficient in sweat glands. The oil keeps his skin soft and prevents it from drying and cracking. It also protects the coat and keeps it water-resistant. When a dog is bathed too often, the natural oil is removed from his skin and the skin and coat become dry. Minute cracks in the skin cause irritation, the dog scratches and bites himself and eczema or other infectious skin ailments may result.

So bathe your dog only when he gets so dirty that it is impossible to clean him any other way. When a bath is necessary, protect the dog's eyes and ears from water before putting him into the tub. Put a drop of castor oil into each eye and plug his ears with cotton. The water should be lukewarm, never hot or cold. Use a special dog soap which does not contain much alkali and rinse all traces of soap from his coat. Then dry him with a thick towel, massage his coat with your hand and brush him. If the day is warm and sunny, let him run outdoors to complete the drying, but if it is cold keep him indoors.

WATCH THE TOENAILS

Many dogs that run on gravel or pavements wear their toenails down so they seldom need clipping. But a dog that doesn't do much running, or runs on grass, will grow long toenails that can be harmful. The long nails will force the dog's toes into the air and spread his feet wide. In addition, the nails may force the dog into an unnatural stance that may produce lameness.

You can control your dog's toenails by cutting them with a special dog clipper or by filing them. Many dogs object to the clipping and it takes some experience to learn just how to do it without cutting into the blood vessels. Your vet will probably examine your dog's nails whenever you bring him in and will trim them at no extra charge. He can show you how to do it yourself in the future. If you prefer, you can file the points off your dog's nails every few weeks with a flat wooden file. Draw the file in only one direction—from

There now—wasn't all that grooming worth it? Remember that trimming your dog is somewhat like clothing yourself—and everyone wants clothes to look well and fit comfortably.

the top of the nail downward in a round stroke to the end of the nail or underneath. You'll need considerable pressure for the first few strokes to break through the hard, polished surface, but then it gets easier.

Incidentally, it's a good idea to keep your young puppy from walking on waxed or slippery floors, as this tends to break down the pasterns.

EYES, EARS AND TEETH

If you notice matter collecting in the corners of the dog's eyes, wipe it out with a piece of cotton or tissue. If there is a discharge, check with your vet.

A Scottish Terrier's ears should receive daily care. Clean the ear to remove any matted dirt or food. Examine the ears and remove all visible wax, using a piece of cotton dipped in a boric acid solution or a solution of equal parts of water and hydrogen peroxide. Be gentle and don't probe into the ear, but just clean the parts you can see. If your dog constantly shakes his head, twitches his ears or scratches them, it is best to have the vet take a look.

If you give your dog a hard chewing bone—the kind you can buy at a pet store—it will serve him as your toothbrush serves you and will prevent the accumulation of tartar on his teeth. However, check his mouth occasionally and take him to the vet if you find collected tartar or bloody spots on his gums.

Your vet will show you how to clip your dog's toenails without cutting into the quick.
This is an essential part of pet care, for overlong nails can cause lameness.

EXERCISE

Your Scottish Terrier will adapt himself to your way of life. If you lead a quiet life with no exercise, so will your Scottie, but it won't be healthy for him. In fact, it may shorten his life. If you have a fenced-in yard where he can run around, fine. If not, long walks, even on a lead, will serve just as well.

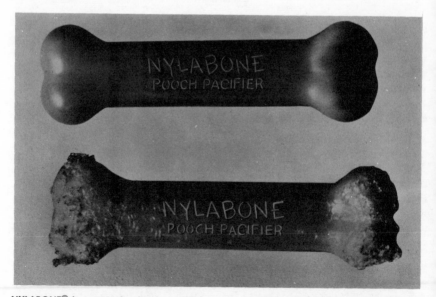

NYLABONE® is a necessity that is available at your local petshop (not in supermarkets). The puppy or grown dog chews the hambone flavored nylon into a frilly dog toothbrush, massaging his gums and cleaning his teeth as he plays. Veterinarians highly recommend this product ... but beware of cheap imitations which might splinter or break.

4. Housebreaking and Training Your Scottish Terrier

The first months of your puppy's life will be a busy time. While he's getting his preventive shots and becoming acquainted with his new family, he should learn the elements of housebreaking that will make him a welcome addition to your home and community.

HOUSEBREAKING THE PUPPY

Housebreaking the puppy isn't difficult because his natural instinct is to keep the place where he sleeps and plays clean. The most important factor is to keep him confined to a fairly small area during the training period. You will find it almost impossible to housebreak a puppy who is given free run of the house. After months of yelling and screaming, you may finally get it through his head that the parlor rug is "verboten," but it will be a long, arduous process.

FIRST, PAPER TRAINING

Spread papers over the puppy's living area. Then watch him carefully. When you notice him starting to whimper, sniff the ground or run around in agitated little circles, rush him to the place that you want to serve as his "toilet" and hold him there till he does his business. Then praise him lavishly. When you remove the soiled papers, leave a small damp piece so that the puppy's sense of smell will lead him back there next time. If he makes a mistake, wash it immediately with warm water, followed by a rinse with water and vinegar. That will kill the odor and prevent discoloration.

It shouldn't take more than a few days for the puppy to get the idea of using newspaper. When he becomes fairly consistent, reduce the area of paper to a few sheets in a corner. As soon as you think he has the idea fixed in his mind, you can let him roam around the house a bit, but keep an eye on him. It might be best to keep him on leash the first few days so you can rush him back to his paper at any signs of an approaching accident.

The normally healthy puppy will want to relieve himself when he wakes up in the morning, after each feeding and after strenuous exercise. During early puppyhood any excitement, such as the return home of a member of the family or the approach of a visitor, may result in floor-wetting, but that phase should pass in a few weeks.

One of the first steps in your pet's education is paper training. Teach him to return to the same area next time by leaving a small damp piece of soiled paper when he's finished.

OUTDOOR HOUSEBREAKING

Keep in mind during the housebreaking process that you can't expect too much from your puppy until he is about 5 months old. Before that, his muscles and digestive system just aren't under his control. However, you can begin outdoor training even while you are paper training the puppy. (He should have learned to walk on lead at this point. See page 46.) First thing in the morning, take him outdoors (to the curb if you are in a city) and walk him back and forth in a small area until he relieves himself. He will probably make a puddle and then just walk around uncertain of what is expected of him. You can try standing him over a piece of newspaper which may give him the idea. Some dog trainers use glycerine suppositories at this point for fast action. Praise the dog every time taking him outside brings results and he'll get the idea. After each meal take him to the same spot.

Use some training word to help your puppy learn. Pick a word that you won't use for any other command and repeat it while you are walking your dog in his outdoor "business" area. It will be a big help when the dog is older if you have some word of command that he can connect with approval to relieve himself in a strange place. You'll find, when you begin the outdoor training, that the male puppy usually requires a longer walk than the female. Both male and female puppies will squat. It isn't until he's quite a bit older that the male dog will begin to lift his leg.

NIGHTTIME TRAINING

If you hate to give up any sleep, you can train your Scottie puppy to go outdoors during the day and use the paper at night for the first few months. After he's older, he'll be able to contain himself all night and wait for his first morning walk. However, if you want to speed up the outdoor training so that you can leave the dog alone in the house with less fear of an accident, keep him confined

Your Scottie puppy will repay your love and patience with loyalty and obedience. Remember that all training takes time, and temper your discipline with plenty of affection.

at night so that he has enough room to move around in his bed but not enough to get any distance away from it. When he has to go, he'll whine loudly enough to attract your attention. Then take him or let him out. You may have to get up once or twice a night for a few weeks but then you can be fairly sure that your puppy will behave indoors—although accidents will happen. Sometimes even a grown dog will suddenly—and for no apparent reason—soil the house, usually the most expensive carpet in it.

Occasionally a puppy that seems to have been housebroken will revert to indiscriminate acts all over the place. If that happens it may be necessary to go back to the beginning and repeat the paper training.

WHEN HE MISBEHAVES

Rubbing a puppy's nose in his dirt or whacking him with a newspaper may make you feel better, but it won't help train the puppy. A dog naturally *wants* to do the right thing for his master. Your job is to show him what you want. If an accident happens, ignore it unless you can catch him immediately and then in a firm tone express your displeasure and take him to the spot he should have used. A puppy has a short memory span, and bawling him out for something that happened a half hour before will have no meaning to him. When he does use the right place, be lavish with praise and petting, but first be sure he has finished. Many a puppy has left a trail of water across a floor because someone interrupted him to tell him how well he was doing.

PUPPY DISCIPLINE

A 6- or 8-week-old puppy is old enough to understand what is probably the most important word in his vocabulary—"NO!" The first time you see the puppy doing something he shouldn't do, chewing something he shouldn't

Mischief is the puppy's middle name, and you never know what's going to happen next. All puppies will chew things but if you give yours toys of his own, he'll be more likely to leave your possessions alone.

Train your Scottie thoroughly so he'll always be welcome whenever you take him traveling and visiting.

chew or wandering in a forbidden area, it's time to teach him. Shout "No" and stamp your foot, hit the table with a piece of newspaper or make some other loud noise. Dogs, especially very young ones, don't like loud noises and your misbehaving pet will readily connect the word with something unpleasant. If he persists, repeat the "No," hold him firmly and slap him sharply across the nose. Before you protest to the A.S.P.C.A. you should realize that a dog does not resent being disciplined if he is doing something wrong and is caught in the act. However, do not chase a puppy around while waving a rolled-up newspaper at him or trying to swat him. Punish him only when you have a firm hold on him. Above all, never call him to you and then punish him. He must learn to associate coming to you with something pleasant.

Every puppy will pick things up. So the second command should be "Drop it!" or "Let go!" Don't engage in a tug-of-war with the puppy, but take the forbidden object from him even if you have to pry his jaws open with your fingers. Many dogs will release what they are holding if you just blow sharply into their faces. Let your dog know that you are displeased when he picks up something he shouldn't.

If you give him toys of his own, he will be less liable to chew your possessions. Avoid soft rubber toys that he can chew to pieces. Don't give him cloth toys, either, as he'll probably swallow pieces and have trouble getting them out of his system. Skip the temptation to give him an old slipper, because it will be hard for him to distinguish between that and a brand-new pair you certainly won't want him to chew. Your pet shop will have some indestructible toys that will be fine for your Scottish Terrier.

However, reconcile yourself to the fact that even with training during puppyhood things will be chewed and damaged, but that's a passing phase in the growth of a dog.

CLIMBING ON FURNITURE

If your Scottie shows a fondness for climbing on furniture, this is another habit you'll have to break early. The upholstery holds the scent of the people he likes, and besides, it's more comfortable than the hard floor or even the carpet. Sometimes verbal corrections will be enough to establish the fact that the furniture is taboo. If not, try putting crinkly cellophane on the furniture to keep him off. If that doesn't work, you can get liquids at your pet store that you can't smell, but whose odor keeps the dog off.

Climbing on furniture is taboo! Be firm and tell him so in no uncertain terms. If your dog has a comfortable place of his own, he won't be so apt to take over your favorite chair.

It may look cute when your dog begs for food, but it's a habit you must not encourage. He has to learn not to disturb you when you're eating, and to eat his food, not yours.

Be consistent in your training. If you're teaching your Scottie not to climb all over you, don't let other members of your family spoil him—even if it's hard to resist.

JUMPING ON PEOPLE

Your Scottish Terrier puppy may try to show his affection by jumping and climbing all over you and everyone else he likes. You may think this is cute while he's still a puppy, but it's a habit you have to break. If you're planning to show him, you won't want him climbing all over the judge in the ring. Besides, not all your friends and relatives are dog lovers and many people prefer to admire dogs from a slight distance. One way to cure the jumping habit is to grab the dog's front paws and flip him backward. Soon he'll develop a more restrained greeting. But he should be patted afterwards so he won't think people are hostile.

And here's a tip on petting the puppy. If everyone pets him on top of the head, as most people do, he may develop the habit of coming over to people with his head down to receive his due. Instead, he should be chucked under the chin. That will keep him in an attractive head-up pose when he greets people—and improve his posture in the show ring or on the street.

5. Obedience Training for Your Scottish Terrier

The purpose of obedience training is not to turn your dog into a puppet but to make him a civilized member of the community in which he will live, and to keep him safe. This training is most important as it makes the difference between having an undisciplined animal in the house or having an enjoyable companion. Both you and your dog will learn a lot from training.

HOW A DOG LEARNS

The dog is the one domestic animal that seems to want to do what his master asks. Unlike other animals that learn by fear or rewards, the dog will work willingly if he is given a kind word or a show of affection.

The hardest part of dog training is communication. If you can get across to the dog what you want him to do, he'll do it. Always remember that your dog does not understand the English language. He can, however, interpret your tone of voice and your gestures. By associating certain words with the act that accompanies them, the dog can acquire a fairly large working vocabulary. Keep in mind that it is the sound rather than the meaning of the words that the dog understands. When he doesn't respond properly, let him know by the tone of your voice that you are disappointed, but follow each correction with a show of affection.

YOUR PART IN TRAINING

You must patiently demonstrate to your dog what each simple word of command means. Guide him with your hands and the training leash through whatever routine you are teaching him. Repeat the word associated with the act. Demonstrate again and again to give the dog the chance to make the connection in his mind. (In psychological language, you are conditioning him to give a specific response to a specific stimulus.)

Once he begins to get the idea, use the word of command without any physical guidance. Drill him. When he makes mistakes, correct him, kindly at first, more severely as his training progresses. Try not to lose your patience or become irritated, and never slap him with your hand or the leash during a training session. Withholding praise or rebuking him will make him feel badly enough.

When he does what you want, praise him lavishly with words and with pats.

When you begin obedience training, your dog must learn to obey your touch. You will have to guide his body through the command motions until he connects the movement with the word.

Don't rely on dog candy or treats in training. The dog that gets into the habit of performing for treats will seldom be fully dependable when he can't smell or see one in the offing. When he carries out a command, even though his performance is slow or sloppy, praise him and he will perform more readily the next time.

THE TRAINING VOICE

When you start training your Scottie, use your training voice, giving commands in a firm, clear tone. Once you give the command, persist until it is obeyed even if you have to pull the dog protestingly to obey you. He must learn that training is different from playing, that a command once given must be obeyed no matter what distractions are present. Remember that the tone and sound of your voice, not loudness, are the qualities that will influence your dog.

Be consistent in the use of words during training. Confine your commands to as few words as possible and never change them. It is best for only one person to carry on the dog's training because different people will use different words and tactics that will confuse the animal. The dog who hears "come," "get over here," "hurry up," "here, Rover" and other commands when he is wanted will become totally confused.

TAKE IT EASY

Training is hard on the dog—and on the trainer. A young dog just cannot take more than 10 minutes of training at a stretch, so limit the length of your first lessons. You'll find that you, too, will tend to become impatient when you stretch out a training session, and losing your temper won't help either of you. Before and after each lesson have a play period, but don't play during a training session. Even the youngest dog soon learns that schooling is a serious matter; fun comes afterward.

Don't spend too much time on one phase of training or the dog will become bored. And always try to end a training session on a pleasant note. If the dog doesn't seem to be getting what you are trying to show him, go back to something simpler that he can do. This way you will end every lesson with a pleasant feeling of accomplishment. Actually, in nine cases out of ten, if your dog isn't doing what you want, it's because you're not getting the idea over to him properly.

An essential part of your dog's training is to keep him from approaching vehicles. If firm words do not do the trick, have a friend seated in the car beside you squirt him with a water pistol as you drive by.

WALKING ON LEAD

"Doggy" people call the leash a "lead," so we'll use that term here. Don't go in for any kind of fancy lead or collar. The best lead for training purposes is the 6-foot webbed-cloth lead, usually olive-drab in color.

As for the collar, you'll need a metal-link collar called a "choke" collar. Even though the name may sound frightening, it won't hurt your dog and it's an absolute *must* in training. It tightens when you snap the lead, eases when you relax your grip. It's important to put the collar on properly. Slide the chain around your dog's neck so that you can attach the lead to the ring at the end of the chain which passes *over*, not under his neck.

Put the collar and lead on the puppy and let him walk around the house first with the lead dragging on the floor. This is just to let him get the feel of the strange object around his neck. But a word of caution for afterward: don't let the dog wander around with the choke collar on. If it's loose he'll lose it, and it's possible for it to catch on any projection and choke him. For his license tag and rabies tag you can get a light leather collar that fits more snugly.

Now, here's a lesson for you. From the start, hold the lead firmly in your right hand. Keep the dog at your left side. You can use your left hand to jerk the lead when necessary to give corrections or to bring the dog closer to you.

Let your Scottie get used to the weight and feel of his training collar before you attempt any lessons with it. Don't let him wear the choke collar when he is alone, for it can catch on things easily.

This little Scottie has learned to sit facing his master and now is ready to do it with the lead off. Sitting is the first position your dog should learn.

Do not *pull* on the lead. Give it a sharp snap when you want to correct the dog, and then release it. The dog cannot learn from being pulled around. He will learn when he finds that doing certain things results in a sharp jerk; doing other things allows him to walk comfortably on lead.

At first, the puppy will fight the lead. He'll probably plant all four feet or his rear end on the ground and wait for your next move. Be patient. Short tugs on the lead will help him learn his part in walking with you. If he gets overexcited, calm him before taking off the lead and collar and picking him up. He must learn there's nothing to fear. (Incidentally, if the lesson is being given on a city street, it might be a good idea to carry some paper to clean up the mess he may leave in his excitement.)

TRAINING TO SIT

Training your dog to sit should be fairly easy. Stand him on your left side, holding the lead fairly short, and command him to "Sit." As you give the verbal command, pull up slightly with the lead and push his hindquarters down (you may have to kneel to do this). Do not let him lie down or stand up. Keep him in a sitting position for a moment, then release the pressure on the lead and praise him. Constantly repeat the command word as you hold him in a sitting position, thus fitting the word to the action in his mind. After a while, he will begin to get the idea and will sit without your having to push his back down. When he reaches that stage, insist that he sit on command. If he is slow to obey, slap his hindquarters with the end of the lead to get him down fast. Teach him to sit on command facing you as well as when he is at your side. When he begins sitting on command with the lead on, try it with the lead off.

THE "LIE DOWN"

The object of this is to get the dog to lie down either on the verbal command "Down!" or when you give him a hand signal, your hand raised, palm toward the dog—a sort of threatening gesture. This is one of the most important parts of training. A well-trained dog will drop on command and stay down whatever the temptation—car-chasing, cat-chasing, or another dog across the street.

Hold the lead in your right hand, and train your dog to go to your left side. Make corrections by jerking the lead with your left hand.

(Above) A well-trained dog will sit on command for three minutes without moving, no matter what distractions are present.

(Below) After your dog has learned the essentials of obedience training, you can teach him to do tricks. To get him in begging position, you may have to hold him at first. A bit of food held high above his head will help this lesson along.

Don't start this until the dog is almost letter-perfect in sitting on command. Then, place the dog in a sit. Force him down by pulling his front feet out forward while pressing on his shoulders and repeating "Down!" Hold the dog down and stroke him gently to let him know that staying down is what you expect of him.

After he begins to get the idea, slide the lead under your left foot and give the command "Down!" At the same time, pull on the lead. This will help get the dog down. Meanwhile, raise your hand in the down signal. Don't expect to accomplish all this in one session. Be patient and work with the dog. He'll cooperate if you show him just what you expect him to do.

THE "STAY"

The next step is to train your dog to stay in either a "sit" or "down" position. Sit him at your side. Give the command "Stay," but be careful not to use his name with that command as hearing his name may lead him to think that some action is expected of him. If he begins to move, repeat "Stay" firmly and hold him down in the sit. Constantly repeat the word "Stay" to fix the meaning of that command in his mind. When he stays for a short time, gradually increase the length of his stay. The hand signal for "stay" is a downward sweep of your hand toward the dog's nose, with the palm toward him. While he is sitting, walk around him and stand in front of him. Hold the lead at first; later, drop the lead on the ground in front of him and keep him sitting. If he bolts, correct him severely and force him back to a sit in the same place.

Use some word such as "Okay" or "Up" to let him know when he can get up, and praise him well for a good performance. As this practice continues, walk farther and farther away from him. Later, try sitting him, giving him the command to stay, and then walk out of sight, first for a few seconds, then for longer periods. A well-trained dog should stay where you put him without moving for 3 minutes or more.

Similarly, practice having him stay in down position, first with you near him, later when you step out of sight.

THE "COME" ON COMMAND

A young puppy will come a-running to people, but an older puppy or dog will have other plans of his own when his master calls him. However, you can train your dog to come when you call him if you begin when he is young. At first, work with him on lead. Sit the dog, then back away the length of the lead and call him, putting as much coaxing affection in your voice as possible. Give an easy tug on the lead to get him started. When he does come, make a big fuss over him and it might help to hand him a piece of dog candy or food as a reward. He should get the idea soon. Then attach a long piece of cord to the lead—15 or 20 feet—and make him come to you from that distance. When he's coming pretty consistently, have him sit when he reaches you.

Don't be too eager to practice coming on command off lead. Wait till you are certain that you have the dog under perfect control before you try calling him when he's free. Once he gets the idea that he can disobey a command to come and get away with it, your training program will suffer a serious setback. Keep in mind that your dog's life may depend on his immediate response to a command to come when he is called. If he disobeys off lead, put the collar back on and correct him severely with jerks of the lead. He'll get the idea.

In training your dog to come, never use the command when you want to punish him. He should associate the "come" with something pleasant. If he comes very slowly, you can speed his response by pulling on the lead, calling him and running backward with him at a brisk pace.

At first, practice the "sit," "down," "stay" and "come" indoors; then try it in an outdoor area where there are distractions to show the dog that he must obey under any conditions.

HEELING

"Heeling" in dog language means having your pet walk alongside you on your left side, close to your left leg, on lead or off. With patience and effort you can train your dog to walk with you even on a crowded street or in the presence of other dogs. However, don't begin this part of his training too early. Normally a dog much under 6 months old is just too young to absorb the idea of heeling.

Put the dog at your left side, sitting. Then say "Heel" firmly and start walking at a brisk pace. Do not pull the dog with you, but guide him by tugs at the lead. Keep some slack on the lead and use your left hand to snap the lead for a correction. Always start off with your left foot and after a while the dog will learn to watch that foot and follow it. Keep repeating "Heel" as you walk, snapping the dog back into position if he lags behind or forges ahead. If he gets out of control, reverse your course sharply and snap him along after you. Keep up a running conversation with your dog, telling him what a good fellow he is when he is heeling, letting him know when he is not.

At first limit your heeling practice to about 5 minutes at a time; later extend it to 15 minutes or a half hour. To keep your dog interested, vary the routine. Make right and left turns, change your pace from a normal walk to a fast trot to a very slow walk. Occasionally make a sharp about-face.

Remember to emphasize the word "Heel" throughout this practice and to use your voice to let him know that you are displeased when he goes ahead or drops behind or swings wide.

If you are handling him properly, the dog should begin to get the idea of heeling in about 15 minutes. If you get no response whatever, if the dog runs away from you, fights the lead, gets you and himself tangled in the lead, it may indicate that he is still young, or that you aren't showing him what you expect him to do.

Practicing 15 minutes a day, in 6 or 7 weeks your pet should have developed to the stage where you can remove the lead and he'll heel alongside you. First try throwing the lead over your shoulder or fastening it to your belt, or remove the lead and tie a piece of thin cord (fishing line will do nicely) to his collar. Then try him off lead. Keep his attention by constantly talking; slap your left leg to keep his attention on you. If he breaks away, return to the collar and lead treatment for a while.

"HEEL" MEANS SIT, TOO

To the dog, the command "Heel" will also mean that he has to sit in heel position at your left side when you stop walking—with no additional command from you. As you practice heeling, force him to sit whenever you stop, at first using the word "Sit," then switching over to the command "Heel." He'll soon get the idea and plop his rear end down when you stop and wait for you to give the command "Heel" and start walking again.

TEACHING TO COME TO HEEL

The object of this is for you to stand still, say "Heel!" and have your dog come right over to you and sit by your left knee in heel position. If your dog has been trained to sit without command every time you stop, he's ready for this step.

Sit him in front of and facing you and step back a few feet. Say "Heel" in your most commanding tone of voice and pull the dog into heel position, making him sit. There are several different ways to do this. You can swing the dog around behind you from your right side, behind your back and to heel position. Or you can pull him toward you, keep him on your left side and swing him to heel position. Use your left heel to straighten him out if he begins to sit behind you or crookedly. This may take a little work, but the dog will understand if you show him just what you want.

THE "STAND"

Your Scottie should be trained to stand on one spot without moving his feet, and should allow a stranger to run his hands over his body and legs without showing any resentment or fear. Use the same method you used in training him to stay on the sit and down. While walking, place your left hand out, palm toward his nose, and command him to stay. His first impulse will be to sit, so be prepared to stop that by placing your hand under his body. If he's really stubborn, you may have to wrap the lead around his body near his hindquarters and hold him up until he gets the idea that this is different from the command to sit. Praise him for standing and walk to the end of the lead. Correct him strongly if he starts to move. Have a stranger approach him and run his hands over the dog's back and down his legs. Keep him standing until you come back to him. Walk around him from his left side, come to heel position, and let the dog sit as you praise him lavishly.

RETRIEVING

It's fun to teach your dog to fetch things on command. Use a wooden dumb-bell, a thick dowel stick or a thin, rolled-up magazine. While you have the dog heeling on lead, hold the object in front of him and tease him by waving it in front of his nose. Then say "Take it" and let him grab it. Walk with him while he's carrying it, and then say "Give" and take it from his mouth. If he drops it first, pick it up and tease him until he takes it again and holds it until you remove it.

With the dog still on lead, throw the object a few feet in front of him and encourage him to pick it up and hold it. If he won't give it up when you want it, don't have a tug-of-war. Just blow into his nostrils and he'll release his hold. Then praise him as if he had given it to you willingly.

Don't become discouraged if he seems slow in getting the idea of retrieving. Sometimes it takes several months before the dog will go after an object and bring it to you, but, with patience and persistence, he'll succeed.

Once he gets the habit of retrieving, try throwing the object over a low hurdle and send him over to pick it up and bring it to you. He should jump the hurdle, get it, jump back over and sit in front of you with the object in his mouth.

Don't expect to accomplish all the training overnight. Generally a dog-training school will devote about ten weeks, with one session a week, to all

When you train your Scottie to jump, you may have to go over the hurdle with him at first to show him what to do.

this training. Between lessons the dogs and their masters are expected to work about fifteen minutes every day on the exercises.

If you'd like more detailed information on training your dog, you'll find it in the pages of HOW TO HOUSEBREAK AND TRAIN YOUR DOG, a Sterling-T.F.H. book.

There are dog-training classes in all parts of the country, some sponsored by the local A.S.P.C.A. A free list of dog-training clubs and schools is available from the Gaines Dog Research Center, 250 Park Avenue, New York, New York.

If you feel that you lack the time or the skill to train your dog yourself, there are professional dog trainers who will do it for you, but basically dog training is a matter of training *you* and your dog to work together as a team, and if you don't do it yourself you will miss a lot of fun.

ADVANCED TRAINING AND OBEDIENCE TRIALS

Once you begin training your Scottie and see how well he does, you'll probably be bitten by the "obedience bug"—the desire to enter him in obedience trials held under American Kennel Club license. Most dog shows now include obedience classes at which your dog can qualify for his "degrees" to demonstrate his usefulness as a companion dog, not merely as a pet or show dog.

The A.K.C. obedience trials are divided into three classes: Novice, Open and Utility.

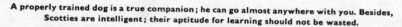
A properly trained dog is a true companion; he can go almost anywhere with you. Besides, Scotties are intelligent; their aptitude for learning should not be wasted.

In the Novice Class, the dog will be judged on the following basis:

Test	Maximum Score
Heel on leash	35
Stand for examination by judge	30
Heel free—off leash	45
Recall (come on command)	30
1-minute sit (handler in ring)	30
3-minute down (handler in ring)	30
Maximum total score	200

If the dog "qualifies" in three different shows by earning at least 50 per cent of the points for each test, with a total of at least 170 for the trial, he has earned the Companion Dog degree and the letters C.D. are entered in the stud book after his name.

After the dog has qualified as a C.D., he is eligible to enter the Open Class competition where he will be judged on this basis:

Test	Maximum Score
Heel free	40
Drop on recall	30
Retrieve (wooden dumbbell) on flat	25
Retrieve over obstacle (hurdle)	35
Broad jump	20
3-minute sit (handler out of ring)	25
5-minute down (handler out of ring)	25
Maximum total score	200

Again he must qualify in three shows for the C.D.X. (Companion Dog Excellent) title and then is eligible for the Utility Class where he can earn the Utility Dog degree in these rugged tests:

Test	Maximum Score
Scent discrimination (picking up article handled by master from group of articles)—Article 1	20
Scent discrimination—Article 2	20
Scent discrimination—Article 3	20
Seek back (picking up article dropped by handler)	30
Signal exercise (heeling, etc., on hand signal only)	35
Directed jumping (over hurdle and bar jump)	40
Group examination	35
Maximum total score	200

For more complete information about these obedience trials, write to the American Kennel Club, 221 Fourth Avenue, New York 3, N. Y., and ask for their free booklet "Regulations and Standards for Obedience Trials." Spayed females and dogs that are disqualified from breed shows because of physical defects are eligible to compete in these trials.

Besides the formal A.K.C. obedience trials, there are informal "match" shows in which dogs compete for ribbons and inexpensive trophies. These shows are run by local Scottish Terrier clubs and by all-breed obedience clubs, and in many localities the A.S.P.C.A. and other groups conduct their own obedience shows. Your local pet shop or kennel can keep you informed about such shows in your vicinity and you will find them listed in the different dog magazines or in the pet column of your local paper.

It's an exciting feat for your Scottie to retrieve an object for you by going over a hurdle. It's excellent exercise as well.

6. Caring for the Female and Raising Puppies

Whether or not you bought your female dog intending to breed her, some preparation is necessary when and if you decide to take this step.

WHEN TO BREED

It is usually best to breed on the second or third season. Plan in advance the time of year which is best for you, taking into account where the puppies will be born and raised. You will keep them until they are at least six weeks old, and a litter of frisky pups takes up considerable space by then. Other considerations are selling the puppies (Christmas vs. springtime sales), your own vacation, and time available to care for them. You'll need at least an hour a day to feed and clean up after the mother and puppies but probably it will take you much longer—with time out to admire and play with them!

CHOOSING THE STUD

You can plan to breed your female about $6\frac{1}{2}$ months after the start of her last season, although a variation of a month or two either way is not unusual. Choose the stud dog and make arrangements well in advance. If you are breeding for show stock, which may command better prices, a mate should be chosen with an eye to complementing the deficiencies of your female. If possible, they should have several ancestors in common within the last two or three generations, as such combinations generally "click" best. He should have a good show record or be the sire of show winners if old enough to be proven.

The owner of such a male usually charges a fee for the use of the dog. The fee varies. This does not guarantee a litter, but you generally have the right to breed your female again if she does not have puppies. In some cases the owner of the stud will agree to take a choice puppy in place of a stud fee. You should settle all details beforehand, including what age the puppies should reach before the stud's owner can make his choice, the possibility of a single surviving puppy, and so on.

If you want to raise a litter just for the fun of it and plan merely to make use of an available male Scottie, the most important point is temperament. Make sure the dog is friendly as well as healthy, because a bad disposition could appear in his puppies, and this is the worst of all traits in a dog destined to be a pet. In such cases a stud fee puppy, not necessarily the choice of the litter, is the usual payment.

The Scottish Terrier Club of America, which is working to keep the quality of Scotties at a high level, is a good source of information when you are looking for a mate for your dog. Many members have stud dogs available, and if you want to breed your female, it will be worth while to join the club. Write to the American Kennel Club for the address and the Secretary's name.

PREPARATION FOR BREEDING

Before you breed your female, make sure she is in good health. She should be neither too thin nor too fat. Any skin disease *must* be cured, before it can be passed on to the puppies. If she has worms she should be wormed before being bred or within 3 weeks afterward. It is generally considered a good idea to revaccinate her against distemper and hepatitis before the puppies are born. This will increase the immunity the puppies receive during their early, most vulnerable period.

The female will probably be ready to breed 12 days after the first colored discharge. You can usually make arrangements to board her with the owner of the male for a few days, to insure her being there at the proper time, or you can take her to be mated and bring her home the same day. If she still appears receptive she may be bred again 2 days later. However, some females never show signs of willingness, so it helps to have the experience of a breeder. Usually the second day after the discharge changes color is the proper time, and she may be bred for about 3 days following. For an additional week or so she may have some discharge and attract other dogs by her odor, but can seldom be bred.

THE FEMALE IN WHELP

You can expect the puppies nine weeks from the day of breeding, although 61 days is as common as 63. During this time the female should receive normal care and exercise. If she was overweight, don't increase her food at first; excess weight at whelping time is bad. If she is on the thin side build her up, giving her a morning meal of cereal and egg yolk. You may add one of the mineral and vitamin supplements to her food, to make sure that the puppies will be healthy. As her appetite increases, feed her more. During the last weeks the puppies grow enormously and she will probably have little room for food and less appetite. She should be tempted with meat, liver and milk, however.

As the female in whelp grows heavier, cut out violent exercise and jumping. Although a dog used to such activities will often play with the children or run around voluntarily, restrain her for her own sake. However, don't eliminate exercise entirely. Walking is very beneficial to the female in whelp, and a daily moderate walk will help her keep up her muscle tone in preparation for the birth.

PREPARING FOR THE PUPPIES

Prepare a whelping box a few days before the puppies are due, and allow the mother to sleep there overnight or to spend some time in it during the day to become accustomed to it. Then she is less likely to try to have her pups under the front porch or in the middle of your bed. The box should have a wooden floor. Sides about a foot high will keep the puppies in but enable the mother to get out after she has fed them. If the weather is cold, the box should be raised about an inch off the floor.

Layers of newspaper spread over the whole area will make excellent bedding and be absorbent enough to keep the surface warm and dry. They should be removed daily and replaced with another thick layer. An old quilt or washable blanket makes better footing for the nursing puppies than slippery newspaper during the first week, and is softer for the mother.

Be prepared for the actual whelping several days in advance. Usually the female will tear up papers, refuse food and generally act restless. These may be false alarms; the real test is her temperature, which will drop to below 100° about 12 hours before whelping. Take it with a rectal thermometer morning and evening, and put her in the pen, looking in on her frequently, when the temperature goes down.

WHELPING

Usually little help is needed but it is wise to stay close to your pet to make sure that the mother's lack of experience does not cause an unnecessary accident. If anything seems wrong, waste no time in calling your veterinarian. You may want his experience in whelping the litter even if all goes well. He will probably prefer to have the puppies born at his hospital rather than to get up in the middle of the night to come to your home. The mother would, no doubt, rather stay at home, but you can be sure she will get the best of care in his hospital.

If the birth takes place at home, be ready to aid the mother when the first puppy arrives, for it could smother if she does not break the membrane enclosing it. She should start right away to lick the puppy, drying and stimulating it, but you can do it with a soft rough towel, instead. The afterbirth should follow the birth of each puppy, attached to the puppy by the long umbilical cord. Watch to make sure that each is expelled anyway, for retaining this material can cause infection. In her instinct for cleanliness the mother will probably eat the afterbirth after biting the cord. One or two will not hurt her; they stimulate milk supply as well as labor for remaining pups. But too many can make her lose appetite for the food she needs to feed her pups and regain her strength. So remove the rest of them along with the wet newspapers and keep the pen dry and clean to relieve her anxiety.

If the mother does not bite the cord, or does it too close to the body, take over the job, to prevent an umbilical hernia. Tearing is recommended, but you can cut it, about two inches from the body, with a sawing motion of scissors, sterilized in alcohol. Then dip the end in a shallow dish of iodine; the cord will dry up and fall off in a few days.

The puppies should follow each other at intervals of not more than half an hour. If more time goes past and you are sure there are still pups to come, a brisk walk outside may start labor again. If she is actively straining without producing a

Prepare a bed for the puppies within sight of the mother. The sides of the box should be high enough to keep the pups in but allow the mother to get away for a while when she wants to. At nursing time the family will be together.

puppy it may be presented backward, a so-called "breech" or upside-down birth. Careful assistance with a well-soaped finger to feel for the puppy or ease it back may help, but never attempt to pull it by force against the mother.

RAISING THE PUPPIES

Hold each puppy to a breast as soon as he is dry, for a good meal without competition. Then he may join his littermates in the basket, out of his mother's way while she is whelping. Keep a supply of evaporated milk on hand for emergencies, or later weaning. A formula of evaporated milk, corn syrup and a little water with egg yolk should be warmed and fed in a doll or baby bottle if necessary. A supplementary feeding often helps weak pups over the hump. Keep track of birth weights and take weekly readings so you will have an accurate record of the pups' growth and health.

After the puppies have arrived, take the mother outside for a walk and drink, and then leave her to take care of them. She will probably not want to stay away more than a minute or two for the first few weeks. Be sure to keep water available at all times, and feed her milk or broth frequently, as she needs liquids to produce milk. To encourage her to eat, offer her the foods she likes best, until she asks to be fed without your tempting her. She will soon develop a ravenous appetite and should have at least two large meals a day, with dry food available in addition.